Sorting the Smoke

Winner of the Iowa Poetry Prize

# Sorting the Smoke

*New & Selected Poems by Conrad Hilberry*

UNIVERSITY OF IOWA PRESS 𝖄 IOWA CITY

University of Iowa Press, Iowa City 52242
Printed in the United States of America
First edition, 1990

Printed on acid-free paper

Library of Congress Cataloging-in-Publication Data

Hilberry, Conrad.
    Sorting the smoke: new and selected poems/by Conrad Hilberry.—
1st ed.
        p.      cm. — (Iowa poetry prize)
    ISBN 0-87745-297-0 (alk. paper), ISBN 0-87745-298-9 (pbk.: alk. paper)
    1. Large type books.   I. Title.   II. Series.
PS3558.I384S67   1990                                    90-35204
811'.54—dc20                                                 CIP

*For Marion*

*Publication of this book was made*

*possible by a generous grant from*

*the University of Iowa Foundation*

# Acknowledgments

I gratefully acknowledge the publications in which these poems originally appeared.

*Beloit Poetry Journal*: "Hamster Cage," "Poet"

*Celery*: "Poem against Celery Hearts and Cream Cheese"

*Chowder Review*: "The Coyote Flower," "A Pleasant Conversation on the Roof," "Street Scene with Fog"

*Field*: "The Chevron," "A Dialogue Concerning the Question Whether a Tennis Ball May Be Said to Hanker for the Other Side of the Net," "For Katharine, 1952–1961," "The Frying Pan," "The House," "The Key," "The Pot Hanger," "The Windlass"

*Green River Review*: "Sonnet"

*Hiram Poetry Review*: "Junior Powell, Sand Gap, Kentucky, with a Borrowed Guitar"

*Kenyon Review*: "Cretan Dawn: A Metaphor," "The Cur," "The Monkey," "Talk," "Toads"

*Lake Superior Review*: "Going Back"

*Michigan Quarterly Review*: "Letter to the North"

*Missouri Review*: "The Double Flail or Double Hook," "The Manure Heap"

*New Lazarus Review*: "Pierre Auguste Renoir, 'Seated Nude' (1916)"

*New Letters*: "Headlights"

*New Yorker*: "Hell-Diver"

*New York Times*: "Sonnet Declining to Write Confessional Poems"

*Ontario Review*: "Skier," "Stop Action" (under the title "Instant Replay")

*Poetry*: "Christmas, Mexico," "The Expatriate," "The Frog," "The Moon Seen as a Slice of Pineapple," "A Procession of Ants, Chanting," "Wise Man" (under the title "A Christmas Poem")

*Poetry Northwest*: "Culvert," "Fisherman," "Script for a Cold Christmas"

*Shenandoah*: "Causation," "Fat," "The Messenger," "North and South," "Rock Video: All Night on the Road," "Zero"
*Sumac*: "Sea"
*Tar River Poetry*: "Five Poems from Crete"
*Thirty-Fourth Street*: "Boy Riding a Bicycle Backwards"
*Three Rivers Poetry Journal*: "The Happy Man"
*Virginia Quarterly Review*: "Explosions at 4:00 A.M.," "Sorting the Smoke"
*Vortex*: "Chloe Courting Nelson Who Stammers," "Sirens"
*Westigan Review*: "Man in the Attic"

*Encounter on Burrows Hill* and *Rust* were published by the Ohio University Press in 1968 and 1974, respectively. All of the *Housemarks* poems were published in a chapbook with that title by Perishable Press, 1980. Most of the *Man in the Attic* poems were published in a chapbook with that title by Bits Press, 1980. The poems from those chapbooks and the "Mexican Poems" were collected in *The Moon Seen as a Slice of Pineapple*, published by the University of Georgia Press, 1984. The housemarks themselves are from Rudolf Koch's *Book of Signs* (Dover Books, 1955). The Mexican illustrations are from Jorge Enciso's *Design Motifs of Ancient Mexico* (Dover Books, 1953). The *Lagoon* poems were published in 1989 in a limited edition handmade by Timothy Barrett, papermaker, Janet Lorence, calligrapher, Bonnie Stahlecker, designer and printer, and Takeshi Takahara, printmaker. The wood engravings from that edition are reproduced here with the gracious permission of Takeshi Takahara.

A Eugene Saxton Fellowship from Harper and Brothers, a Chapelbrook Foundation grant, two fellowships from the National Endowment for the Arts, two residencies at the MacDowell Colony, and sabbatical leaves from Kalamazoo College provided time for the writing of many of these poems.

# Contents

# Sorting the Smoke

# Self-Portrait as Bank Teller

As my fingers almost touch the fingers
reaching under the bars but touch instead
checks and deposit slips—as my hand reaches

for the other hand and almost touches it—
I feel the float, the moment out of time
when money passed from hand to hand forgets

the pale depositer and rains interest
on the banking clerk himself—on me
as I hit the date stamp and slide the bills

into the drawer. All day, between the hand in
and the hand out, I sense the float distilling
its small rain about me, between words in

and words out, I hear the silence adding its six
percent, the miracle of commerce that blesses
even those who sign no checks themselves.

# The Messenger

*for John Spencer*

My office door opens a crack
and a skinny arm reaches,
hands me an envelope,
and is gone. The yellow sheet
is blank, except for a fine-
lined map, and John's name.
I follow the grey line up
Academy Street as the day
thins and fades. No dogs
bark in the distance. I walk
as though I had no body,
nothing stored in the folds
and fat. Jeff Smith crosses
ahead of me, vectoring off
to his own house. No smells
rise from kitchens. My wife
drives past, the car moving
on the bricks without
a sound. I recognize her
as I might recognize
a name in a list of names.
At the corner, the map turns
like a line of reasoning
and draws me down Monroe Street.

"Hello, John," I say,
rousing him. "Con,"
he says, his eyes still shut.
I touch his bald head,
now crossed by a scar,

and talk a while. He shakes,
sobbing, almost soundless,
crying for everything
his body remembers and can
no longer sort into words.
Now the world rushes back,
voices of Annabelle and Jean,
the smell of dinner, the past
crowded with talk, affection,
ideas fleshy as figs, the weight
of students tangled in
their lives. For myself, too,
the rush of longing, the thick
taste of loves and deaths,
the purple of a Spanish sky,
the pulse of train wheels,
a daughter who should not
have died.

      Outside the window,
the Western Union man
pedals his balloon-tired bike
up Monroe, his face flushed,
his uniform splashed with salt,
his breath blowing in a white
cloud around his ears.

# Talk

Without the distraction
of meaning, we notice
the fact: talk.

A table of Finns,
two Greeks across
a counter, a knot

of Germans waiting
for a bus—what
could they be saying

that would keep them
leaning so intently
toward each other?

# Five Poems from Crete

## Heraclitus' Bird

*The transformations of fire are, first of all, sea;*
*and half of the sea is earth, half lightning-storm.*
                    —Heraclitus

A bird, put together
the way that sentence
is, would be extinct
by now. But Heraclitus'
ostrich, being made of
words, still flaps
its curious wings
and sprints along
the road above the sea,
looking backward
at the lightning-storm,
while travellers stop
their motorbikes
and stare.

Gulls

I brought these gulls with me
up from the harbor. I am
honored to have them circling
over me, here on the cliff,
remembering that Roethke wore
a crown of birds for a moment
once on a point of land.
Hovering and calling, they
hang in the middle distance.
I like their banks and turns,
their half-tucked legs, the small
adjustments of their wings
that keep them steady. But gulls
are gulls. Behind them, a high
cirrus melancholy drifts
against pure blue, and I
long to try that thin air.
But the sky is seamed with
the crossing paths of birds.
Like Gulliver, I am held
by the fine threads of their flight,
by their tight cries explaining
*sky, sky, sky, sky, sky, sky.*

Flora

Thin-petalled poppies,
blue kalva silvestris,
purple orchids on
a straight stem,
faskómilo to settle
the stomach, thistles,
vetches, daisies—
these, too, are words
of a sort, something
between us and the rock.


Tertium Quid in a Trench Coat

Subject and object, imagination
and reality—these opposites
account for everything. But who's
this tertium quid, carrying
papers from both countries,
hanging around harbors and landing
fields, betraying secrets both ways?

An Armload of Groceries


Here you come, walking downhill
from town, into the sea wind,
with bags in your arms—tomatoes,
perhaps, and cheese and oranges.
I walk to meet you. Still fifteen
feet apart, we start talking—
not aiming to clarify or convince,
just talking, saying what happened,
swinging the incense of words
down the sloping street to lunch.

# Cretan Dawn: A Metaphor

After sunset, men
in black pants, black
sweaters and scarves ran
from streets back

of the wharves, ran
the lost narrow
paths on the mountain,
finding the shadow

of rocks, keeping down.
Now, the sun drops
its Aryan
paratroops,

blond and brazen,
to burn the crops
and seize the main
road on the coast.

It is seven
o'clock. The mist
lies sullen
here in the inlet,

still loyal to night.

## Paros in the Rain

The sky covers the bay like a lid
and drips. Low mountains
have faded to grey, growing here
and there a half-built house,
steel rods rising from concrete

like assertions going beyond
the evidence. We won't go in
to town today, won't take the boat
to Antiparos and the caves.
With the sun gone, everything

we sailed away from seeps back:
the blank present tense, mirrors,
the indoor loneliness of Americans
whose only window is a television.
On the news, President Arias

offers a simple, sensible
plan for peace—and the world
is so astonished they give him
the Nobel Prize. Even good news
brings on this lethargy and gloom.

Still, we've rented the motorbike.
Two ancient tourists with spectacles
and helmets, we chug upright into
the drizzle. A Greek man in a blue
doorway waves both arms and grins.

# Fire

*Fire coming on will discern and catch up with all things.*
                                                    —Heraclitus


For the first time since I was ten,
there's nothing I have to do. Morning

rolls over and it is afternoon.
Afternoon rubs suntan oil

on its chest, lies back, and pulls a hat
over its face. Small waves ease up

around its ankles, and it is evening.
Bye and bye, the full moon walks in

asking no questions. Love and justice
lost track of me as I slipped

through the time zones: in the Cretan wind
what happens happens. Yet the moon

rises and falls when she said she would.
It is dawn. On this rocky spit

at the world's end, fire comes on:
the poppy blazes and the sea smokes.

## Sorting the Smoke

*If all things were turned to smoke, the nostrils*
*would distinguish them.*

—Heraclitus

### 1

In the thick smoke, the nostrils lift
and sniff: cedar roof beams, the soggy
blanket that has hung all these years
in the shed, paint from kitchen chairs,
the singed fur of cat and the flesh
of cat, and the loquat tree by the wall,
and thyme, and books in grandfather's room
and his wool robe and the mattress
and grandfather and the coarse grasses
behind the house. Whose nostrils are
we speaking of, downwind of the fire?

### 2

The smoke billows in dark eddies
as though the world hid just behind it,
as though it might drift off, and the road,
the child in white, the blind horse tied
to the cypress tree might reappear
like fishing boats still hung with mist.
But no. The smoke does thin and swirl
and fade, but nothing steps out, no shapes
re-form in the middle distance;
only the emptiness comes clear
to the watcher who himself is smoke.
A faint smell lingers, and the nostrils
sort it into everything that was.

# North and South

We sons of German mothers honor
small perfections: a well-cooked flan,
the soundless turning of a wheel,
a mitred corner, the polish on

an auto grill. The philodendron
answers the thrown curve of its pot.
Poised for verse, we ask if rhyme
would be appropriate or not.

As for landscapes, we assume
that well-hedged fields will fall into
a satisfactory pattern—and
of course they do, they do.

Yet looking south, we see countries
where sullen passion and poverty,
heat, recklessness, and sloth somehow
are granted cypresses and sea,

ravines, hills ripe as women. Unjustly,
trees of convenient height hand olives
to whoever has the enterprise
to reach for them, and a vine gives

wine by the glass. A painter who never
learned to draw stumbles on sunlight,
splashes it on with loose, raw strokes—
and gets the whole thing right.

# Rock Video: All Night on the Road

It's so far down, all I can hear is
the bass line, terribly slow, waves sliding in
and crashing against the cliff, slow as days,
as seasons. All afternoon, here on the headlands,
I listen to the undertow. The gulls'
intricate turns must be the tenor sax
working over the bass. Rock music.
And here's the video to go with it:
semis on the interstate, an endless line
of them, through a long lens, moving toward me,
topping the speed limit yet coming on slowly,
mysteriously. They have been all night
on the road, radios blaring to keep them awake,
and now, too tired to care, the first driver
swings his rig sideways into a long,
slow skid, toppling, then crashing on the rocks.
After him, the next driver and the next,
easing into a skid, the momentum of all
those miles coming sidelong into the cliff
and shattering, trucks marked X-Press, Safeway,
Bekin, Atlas, CocaCola crashing
below me. It must be trick photography,
yet I watch in horror, calmly, caught
in the rhythm, wanting to drive one
of those sleepy rigs, turn the wheel
to throw tractor and trailer into the long
skid, then ease my shoulders and lean back
as the deep music moves into the cliff.

# The Woman from Chiapas

Except for the eyes, who would know her?
Eyes narrow and still and hard in a broad
face, eyes young enough to be resigned
and furious at the same time. The mother
from Chiapas—we guess she's seventeen—
holds her child in a blue rebozo, his
nose flat against her blouse, his face
dark. The child, when he is grown,

may become a storyteller, a man
that men and women follow—grave,
graceful, and forgiving. But the woman
has seen grace terrify the bosses
and make them brutal. She looks at us
steadily. She foresees and does not forgive.

## A Pleasant Conversation on the Roof

Talking here on the roof, we pay no attention
to the egrets twanging their hoarse chords
nor to the distant bus stammering up
a mountain road. We are naming friends—

Tom whose script is actually being shot and David
who went north and married that woman—
not thinking of the wind that started in
the flume of a dry canyon, gathered voices

as it fell, and now rushes over us
like regret. We talk of Nancy's daughters,
Carla and Jenny, growing up in this strange town
of fireworks and barren hills and discos.

From the pecan tree behind us, a grackle calls
*Oye*, but we are not listening. The air
carries a hint of sulphur, almost imperceptible
like the faint rustle of the past moving

the leaves. We do not notice the distant hills
of our own breathing, nor the stomach and kidney
and colon doing their ordinary work
nor the slight fear rising from the turned earth

of childhood. We are talking about Lou who studied
theology in a Mexican seminary.
The insistent honking of egrets does not define
itself as a hankering in the air between us.

Like children following a trail of crumbs,
we attend to one word after another
as though they would lead us home. But while
we are looking down, flocks of birds circle

and alight. They eat the crumbs. Now which way,
Gretel? We look up to find the sky vanished.
Children baffled in a dark wood, we stumble
in the underbrush, search, turn, and are lost.

A snow-white bird sings from a bough, and having
no other guide, we follow it, parting the ferns
with our thighs, climbing a long hill until
we smell the heavy fragrance of an oven.

# Causation

In the north, we live at sea level,
a city of swamps and celery, paper
factories and pharmaceuticals.
As clouds stay all winter, resting on
the housetops, so causation hangs
above us, accounting for everything.
And yet we believe we choose: choose
cautiously, choose our causes.
Here, two thousand miles south
a blue and distant sky holds all
events like a hand of five-card draw,
discarding, betting, spreading cards
on the table at a single stroke.
Bulls running the streets. One boy
is gored, but who can find a reason
when three hundred others run unhurt?
In a country like this, twenty-six
years ago, a girl leaned from a train,
was killed: an accident, with causes.
An accident that would not have happened
in a cautious country. Do I come
here to find her, somehow, in this
reckless air, as in the church
of Nuestra Señora de la Salud
men and women pray for remedy
to the same God who crippled them?
I drag a lame hip and sore heart
into the scorching sunlight where pain
is not muffled in reasons but clangs

and booms on the hour, the half hour,
the quarter hour, where women nod
*bueno día*, letting the final *s*'s dissolve
in the bitter saliva behind their teeth.

# Zero

**1**

Nothing with a rim
of salt, the button-hole
through which you may
put on, take off,
the noiseless hum
of blood in the inner
ear, a nod, a gesture
empty now but ready if
significance should come.

**2**

Although I lack 5's flying
hair and the tongue of 3
in an open jaw, I have my uses.
I keep you in the high rent
district left of the decimal
point, or I officiate
at your diminishing. My
emptiness invites an echo,
a resonance of bells or cocks
or frenzied dogs on rooftops.
I am the hollow in the street
where water gathers after
the rain, reflecting
the rear lights of a car.

3

The planets' orbits, which once
were circular, are now
elliptical, a sign
of perfect nihilation,
zilch, a universe
of absences. Venus

writes her mark on the sky,
an oval like lips pursed
for a kiss. But no one
looking up can see
those lips. They are a zero
pencilled on nothing,

the dry idea of a kiss.

4

In this binary age, we are
minimalists: one or zero.
We give the world itself
a fifty-fifty chance. Our
afternoons on the Grande Jatte
dissolve to tiny colored
zeros whenever we come
close enough to touch.

## 5

We can no longer believe that evil is
an accident to be explained, a terrible
falling off from an ordained perfection.
Evil, now, is where we start. The garden.
The key of C Major. Red, yellow, and blue.
Deception, violation, greed. The matrix
is a cyclone fence, zeros with their elbows
linked like riot police. From this ground come
the sweet conjunctions that astonish us.

## 6

Zero, I suppose, cannot be filled—
except as a painter from Guerrero fills
the oval side of a fish with pelicans
in flight and turtles and the crescent moon.

If I could, I'd crowd this closed
parenthesis with wife and daughters,
friends—crowd all of them around
the kitchen table here in privation's
house, where meaning may be traded
for a lovely emptiness, a sudden O
our tongues have lifted out from all
the phonemes clamoring on the street.

from *Encounter on Burrows Hill* (1968)

# Hamster Cage

Quiet, the children look on
As the small mammal
Nesting in chips and lettuce
Gives birth, bloody and natural.
They see how it's done,

Watch her licking them clean—
But more than licking, the teeth
Working on the diminutive head,
Back, haunch, one then both,
Till blood and a tuft of down

Are the only sign.
Drawn by cries, parents disbelieve,
Then, believing, go silent,
Send children off, remove
The unspeakable mother whose calm

Jaw mocked their bargain:
Treadmill, breadcrumbs, suet
In exchange for a clean bit
Of wilderness, a pet,
A cage of instruction.

# Sirens

Like the distant crying of someone else's child,
Sirens rise and fall, urgent,
Across the dark city. Accident
Or arson, bad news speaks from this tangled
Whine. Yet to my ear the far howl
Comes in welcome as music on the night air.
Is it because it says flame still can stir
In the dry boards, peel plaster down, call
Out the trucks, the leaping-nets, the hoses
Flat on the street until they spring
With juice and issue a splendid Gulliver douse
To the wind? Or because, while flaming birds are whistling
Colors somewhere into the dark of windows,
In this house, for this hour, all fires are sleeping?

# Poet

*If the poet is tone-deaf as to sounds, it is best to rely upon the phonetic symbols above each group of rhyming words in the rhyming dictionary that terminates this book, or upon dictionary markings. Many people can not distinguish the obvious difference in sounds between this pair of words, which do not rhyme:*

north, forth.

*Take away the* th *sound, and many people still hear no difference between this pair of words, which do not rhyme:*

nor, fore.

*Take away the* r *sound, and some people still hear no difference between this pair of words, which do not rhyme:*

gnaw, foe.

Gnaw *plus* r *plus* th *can not rhyme with* foe *plus* r *plus* th.
    —Clement Wood, *The Complete Rhyming Dictionary and Poet's Craft Book*


O, lucky poet tone-deaf
As to something else than sounds!
(Tone-deaf to the turning leaf?
Tone-deaf to autumn wounds?)

He walks in step with what he hears.
Keeps both beat and pitch;
Without a circumflex he fares
*Foe* plus *r* plus *th*.

This striding, compass-perfect poet
Never strays to *know-earth*
Impeccably he sounds the note
And sets his foot to *gnaw-earth*.

# Hell-Diver

*hell-diver*, n. *A dabchick or other small grebe.*
               *—Webster's Collegiate Dictionary*

On the glebe
The small grebe,
Kin to the widgeon,
Moves with the gait
Of a celibate
Pigeon,
The tread
Of a scoter
Whose motor
Is dead—
He's a sick
Dabchick.

But afloat he is yare,
And steep as a merlin
Stoops in air
He drops through seas
That corals curl in,
Plummets,
The plumed, bizarre fish,
Headlong as though he's
Sighted a starfish
And aims to wive her,
The hell-diver.

# March Birthday

Two starlings sail down
A wind, catapult
Above the crown
Of oak and elm, vault

Half the sky on headlong
Air, then suddenly
Swing
About and light on an ash tree.

So on my March day
I turn upwind and hang
And sway
A time to hear the clang

Of the sky's bell and watch
The low clouds ride, the willow
Weave and reach,
Bearing the year's first yellow.

The starlings and I
Mimic the redbird's song
But dry,
Shrill, getting it wrong.

Perch, whistle awhile, then fling
Out, arch a down-wind way
On black wings
To celebrate a borning day.

# Chloe Courting Nelson Who Stammers

"That's all right, Nelson, take your time.
The night's out walking, and the plum
Will lean on the porch till you can say it out.
Besides I like to watch your tongue
Arch and fight

Like a caught fish. The others pour such thin
Streams, it's good to see a turn
Of muscle there, even if it's stuck—
At least it doesn't skin
A rainbow slick

On the pond. Nelson, you know what
Your words do? They rise in your throat
And your Adam's apple punches them down
Like drowned kittens that float
Up and up again.

Kittens—or weasels. How come they sit
Right there in your throat? Mostly men silt
The beasts in at the bottom, safe
As bones—Snapper the old dog under the dirt—
Safe as a laugh

In the river mud. Nelson, I like
You. I won't care. Take the crick
Out of your throat and let the words tumble
Like stuff over the dam: a snake,
A catfish, windfall

Apples, weeds, an eel, a soggy stick.
Here, a kiss. To draw the words. To suck
The staggering fruit. Dear Nelson!"
He held her while the plum breathed back
The easy run

Of wind in the night's throat and the river
Spilled its casual freight, leaves and litter,
Like seeds tossed over a shoulder. She
Waited. His lips, moving like water,
Spoke only, "Chloe."

from *Rust* (1974)

# A Thin Song for a Girl

Your eyes
Worry with words
And the curl of
Numbers, fearing
A wrong turn.

I wish I could say
Unlearn them—
The world's skin
Is unlettered
And $n$ is no
Count.

I wish I could say
The rain erases
Numbers and
Rinses names
Away.

     But
It would not
Be true. A stand
Of oak speaks
With ten thousand
Green tongues
Scattering words
Like a blur
Of blackbirds.

Even Brushy Fork
Multiplies and
Divides on its wet
Slate. The dark
Marks will be there,
Mumbling their mysteries.

Forgive them
If you can.
Already you know
Round numbers
By their tuck and roll.
Behind the bars
Of a lined page
You know a mean
Wind by its
Garlic breath.

# The Day of the First Draft Lottery

### 1

My daughters make wheel and spokes
In the snow of the park:
One fox, two geese. At 4:30
It is dusk. An early moon watches
The game with half an eye.

### 2

March 1. My number: 108. Called
Except for a steel hip
And 41 spruce trees
41 hamburger buns skidding for grackles on snow crust
41 daughters, wives
41 bicycle tubes patched and pumped
41 pork loins @ 89¢
41 Yeats poems ranting and carolling in a mad tenor.

### 3

I hung at the sky's end
Of a seesaw one summer, then
Down while my brother rose,
A kite taking the wind.
Always, the sudden lull
At the top where the green air
Holds breath in its hands
And arms walk with no elbows.

In that still circle, a starling
Whistles the strict sound
Of a name: mine, a fox's, a crow's.

4

After Labor Day, bare pipes
Stand footed in concrete,
Their wings and
Genitals removed.
Iron steps rise from the snow
But a child climbs to a sudden
Emptiness.

5

If only the vowels would stop rising
And falling, I could say it out.
I can hear it shuffling on a spruce
Somewhere behind my head. But
*e*, *y*, and *i* wobble on legs too thin for a bird.
I cannot give my name.

6

Night. Children race
In a ring, one fox, two geese,
Till the spokes blur
And the red and black of the wheel
Throws numbers into the trees.

Calling her sister's name
Clear as the moon, a girl
Ducks into the still hub.
Then daughters spin out from the rim,
Slivers of words in the Christmas snow.

# Sea

The sea breaks. I turn
And take it, a monk's
Hood over my head,
Then dive into a wave,
Feeling the heave and slough
As tangled water passes.

Out beyond breakers, water swells
And settles, taking a deep breath
For the landing. Buoyed by this depth
I let all sinews go, sell these bones
To the sea—two good shoulders
And a bad leg. Let water take

Them, salvage or discard them
As it will. No time but this.
No obligation, no comfort, no
Accomplishment. No person but
The sea with its cold hands. The sun,
Too far, touches no part of me.

Without my willing it, the sea
Brings from its hoard a salt recollection:
The bitter ache for a daughter
Dead, a girl who walked weightless
In my love. Her absence rises
And falls with me in the heavy water.

Shouts from the beach. Another girl,
Alive, runs to taste the cold

In a single dash and fall.
She swims out, and I crawl
Over the curl of breakers
Toward the lame and slippery shore.

# For Katharine, 1952–1961

### 1

Your flesh is melted, I suppose,
To Indiana clay. Only your bones
Attend that deep box. Graceful
They must be, even now.

### 2

Dead as many years
As you lived. If a child
Grows back down, a year
For a year, you are a hard
Birth to be taken in,
A conception, and nothing.

### 3

Katharine, we die.
My father is dead
And his brother.
Some of us grow down
While we live.
     *What? Am I telling you*
*About death?*
    This is what I know:
You visited the neighbors'
Cats. In the park, you
Climbed down rocks
To fern and twisting
Water. Once we camped

By a soggy little lake, drove
Home in the rain, late,
Singing, the lights of the towns
Blurred and wonderful in the wet
Pavement. We planted
Corn, do you remember?
And in August felt
The full ears, husked
Them, broke the sweet
Kernels with our teeth.

You grew so easily
There seemed no other way.
Your voice held out
Its hands, palms up.

This motion, this poise—
Broken to wet bones in a box.

4

On this day of your death,
We love. The steep
Water of your making
Is still green—
And will be, will be.
The fern, the falls,
The keeping on.

## Junior Powell, Sand Gap, Kentucky, with a Borrowed Guitar

He picks a fast passage, waking
December flies on the ceiling.
Listens.
Tunes the first string, low

High   low. Tries an A chord.
And D. He picks his passage again
Untangling it
From the strings, offering

That ornament to a bare room
And a long night. That riff is his
Employment.
He winds two strings down

And up again. One of them whines
Lost. He smiles. Worries the knob.
Nothing here
To tune by. Outside a pile

Of coal squats in the path
Blocking the way. He tries D
Building it
From the bottom up, sixteen inches

On center, a life. The top notes
Falter and warp. He winds down
Three strings
And starts over. Smiles. Uncertain

Intervals hollow out the time,
A vacancy between drops of rain.
You know
How to tune this son of a bitch?

Jimmy knows but he's gone. All tunes going
Or gone, roads turning back
On themselves.
You know how to play poker?

We play five card draw with no money, showing
Our hands after the draw. A pair of fives
Takes it
If there was anything to take.

## Boy Riding a Bicycle Backwards

Perched on the handlebars, you are living
Backwards, pedalling the wrong way,
Pulling left for a right turn.

You are writing
A crooked poem
From the bottom
Up, not even
Turning
To see where
It will start.

# Sonnet Declining to Write Confessional Poems

Left to myself, I flatten to clear water,
Giving back grey-green rocks, low
Clouds, a lighthouse that marks the slow
Traffic of a gull and a freighter.
I breathe wild onion cut by a sickle bar
On shore. The mower cools a beer in shallow
Water, leans for lunch on a shadow
Whose shape is mine. I have no character.

Must all songs twist out of the conches of our
Ears, roaring the inward salt and blood?
The real sea keeps a dour
Beat, scraping what music it can out of flood
And ebb. It never asked me to pick
A sea riff on the five strings of my neck.

## Four Kentucky Poems

### Rust

Mountains kneel to drink
Humping their backs over cupped hands.
Whatever sits still
On these lovely slopes
Corrodes
And whatever moves
Must find its own gait
With no instruction
But the running of the rain.

Going Back


Going back to a garage that smells
Of fertilizer and motor oil

Or to an upstairs room where
You lay awake to the rain
And the moving cars—

Going back, you do not expect
Pleasure. You hope to find

That words broken open
Spill on a dry tongue
A taste they have been saving.

You hope to find
Water still cold as iron.

Rivers

Whether it rains or not
Brushy Fork slides and sidles
Over its broad slate bed.
Water oozes from the fat
Rocks, coal juice dribbling
From the side of a mouth.
It brings no traffic
But it has studied two ridges
And a valley, and its word is good.
If you are going to Silver Creek,
It will show you the way.

  * * *

Knowing rivers, you know the slope and bias
Of the earth's body. You know how the land lies.

  * * *

The only river I could name
Was the Detroit River, making
The slow commuter run from Grosse
Pointe to Lincoln Park and back.
It lapped the sludgy banks of Belle
Isle and the pier where Bob-Lo Boats
Came in, blowing a calliope of promises.

Culvert


Brushy Fork moves
Over slick shale, picking
The scabs of fallen trees, narrows
To the dark hole of a culvert
Where its coughing echoes
Back on itself,
Matter deep in the throat.
But always moving. Under the dry road
Water rattles in the corrugated pipe
Until coughing settles into
Something like health—a meadow,
The gentle seepage of cow dung.
Not pure. Not your New Hampshire
Brook. But moving. A new smell,
Strange land under the flowing body.

from *Housemarks* (1980)

*These housemarks from Rudolf Koch's* Book of Signs *are ancient marks used by peasants to identify themselves and their property. According to Koch, they were embroidered on rugs or cloths, carved into lottery sticks, punched into the iron of farm implements, branded into the hides of domestic animals or the horns of cattle, painted on the fleeces of sheep, and even ploughed into fields.*

## The Chevron

This is my sign, the pitch
of my tent on low ground.
It is the march up the mountain
and the march down. It is
a crossroads without a choice.
It is my past and my future
leaning together like cornstalks
after the rain. This broken
stick confers no honor,
but it has marked me.
It has stolen the comfort
of a bare sleeve.

## The Key

As geraniums appear over doors,
beside driveways, on porches
and window sills, so the city
is blooming with locks.
They hang from bicycle wheels
languid as orchids. On each
jewelry box, diary, and travelling
case grows the tiny bouquet
of a lock. Bedroom doors wear them
like a rose in the navel.

Imagine, then, how modest
I may be, how gentlemanly.
I seldom mention my mark.
When the need arises, you will,
somehow, have guessed it.

## The Double Flail or Double Hook

Separate, we are a pair of sevens
standing in the rain. But crossed
by a single purpose, we brand
our house with angles. Fierce
sticks, we flail the chaff away,
then flail on until the grain
itself is broken and blown.
We face opposite directions,
sharpening our hooks. Then
we slash, slash away limbs,
faces, genitals until we are
one figure, relentless and pure.
Double flail, double hook.
In our dark geometry, we lean
toward each other and away.

## The Windlass

In me, opposites face each other
like poker players drawn to the table
yet holding their cards to themselves.
Spades, diamonds, hearts, clubs.
The chips meet in the middle.
One man deals the cards, clockwise,
into four piles, their backs
patterned like four turtles floating
in a slow eddy. The players are skillful
and cautious; the money rises and falls
gently in front of them. It is late,
but no one moves to leave. Finally,
they notice that all of them are
losing. The game grows silent, except
for the creak of the table, turning.

## The House

The sides of my house are all
of a length, achieving a simple
symmetry, a shape basic
to the sciences. An ancient
sign, it stands for fire rising.

What the dark line may be, below,
I couldn't say—a slab
under the building. Perhaps
it is the log the fire feeds on
or perhaps a drunken uncle
who must lie outside the door.
What could it be, this heavy stroke
below the pure triangle, this long
tongue that never learned to speak?

## The Manure Heap

If you are looking for breasts like two pink
sheep nibbling their way up the hillside,
you have come to the wrong place.
This is no haystack or feather bed. Here,
the heat rises straight from the ground,
and the scent is not imported. My mark
is a plain one, broad as my skirt, but
you will remember it. You are talking
to a woman who will be here tomorrow,
tough as grass, and when you shake the reins
and drive out the gate, the spreader
will be heaped with a rich crop.

## The Frying Pan

My mark is my confusion.
If I believe it, I am
another long-necked girl
with the same face.
I am emptiness reflected
in a looking glass, a head
kept by a collar and leash,
a round belly with something
knocking to get in.

But cross the handle
with a short stroke
and I am Venus, the old
beauty. I am both the egg
and the pan it cooks in,
the slow heat, the miraculous
sun rising.

## The Pot Hanger

It's not all bad, having buck teeth
and a name like Pot Hanger. No one
can think of you as a quarterback
or a lover or president of the bank,
so you try something else, something
no one particularly wants. You're
good at it, maybe, and get your name
on an invention or a new species
of mushroom. As it turns out,
even a girl can enjoy your company.
And everything that happens is
a surprise—as though you, a catfish,
should find yourself leaning your elbows
on the bank, giving a bit of advice
to the Corps of Engineers, then swimming
off to New Orleans with a brown trout.

from *Man in the Attic* (1980)

# Stop Action

*for Brownie Galligan*

Slowly as in an underwater dance
the shortstop dips to take the ball
on a low hop, swings back his arm, balancing
without thought, all muscles intending
the diagonal to the first baseman's glove.

As the ball leaves his hand, the action stops—
and, watching, we feel a curious poignancy,
a catch in the throat. It is not this play
only. Whenever the sweet drive is stopped
and held, our breath wells up like the rush

of sadness or longing we sometimes feel
without remembering the cause of it.
The absolute moment gathers the surge
and muscle of the past, complete,
yet hurling itself forward—arrested
here between its birth and perishing.

## Man in the Attic

He hoists himself into the attic and crawls
toward the eaves where he knows the leak must be.
He hears the rain rush up the roof, then down
and over the edge. He has a plan. He will catch

the water in a cake pan before it seeps
into the bedroom ceiling. Already the plaster
swells to an enormous sore and drips
sometimes with yellow matter. On his belly

now he pushes the pan ahead of him,
scraping his head on a nail. Feeling back
into the dark for the wet place, he finds
splinters, crumbs of plaster, and a soft fur

of dirt. In the acute angle of the eaves,
the boards are warped and vaguely damp,
but there is no drip, nothing you could catch
in a pan. Further and further back: nothing.

When he thinks of himself wedged in under the slope
of his own attic, impaled on roofing nails—
a grown man stretched out on his belly
contriving to catch rain in a cake pan—

he almost cries. Below, he knows, his wife
watches the swollen ceiling drain on their bed.

# Fisherman

Wet to the knees, the fisherman studies the twist
and fall of water then drops the fly in a pool
beyond a log. He takes the subtle trout.
Like finds like. His hand and eye are cousin
to the fish, that canny bit of river.

A feeling stirs in him like a thin mist
on the water. It rises with his breath
penetrant as shame, he thinks, or regret.
Nothing to do with the trout, it is a smell
almost remembered—the heaviness of an attic
or the musk of leaves. His heart is hidden in it.

Hand and eye know their trade, but the body is
the whole canyon, the river falling, ignorant,
over rocks and debris, over the fisherman's
boots, over the precise scales of the trout.
It is osier, marsh grass, the broken cliff,
vague browns and greys and greens rumbling
in their sleep. It will not rise to the lure.

## Pierre Auguste Renoir, "Seated Nude" (1916)

We had forgotten, almost, what a woman looks like. This is
unmistakably a woman, her flesh and her thoughts both heavy.
Her friends are washing themselves in the river—one scrubbing a
knee, the other drying the back of her neck or fixing her hair,
hoping perhaps that someone is watching through the yellow-
green shrubbery. But the seated nude hopes nothing. It is a hot
day. She is rid of her clothes at last, and rid of talk. Her shoulders
let their weight down into her arms. If she were not so young,
gravity would carry all her heaviness into her hips, but as it is, her
breasts have a mind of their own, looking us in the eye. A minute
ago, she pushed the reddish hair back off her forehead, uncovering
an earring. Her mind is not on that. She stares past us, to our
right, not seeing us—or wishing she did not see us—her eyes
settling on the thick strokes of leaf, bark, and water behind us.

Now, the other bathers dry themselves to go. Since she ignores us,
we know we too should draw away, so she may have the canvas to
herself. Yet we stay. After all, Renoir is here, the old man, painting
her into the slopes and shades of her flesh, feeling its heaviness,
her heaviness, his hand exuberant in the contours of her body.

## Street Scene with Fog

The hiss of the storm door trails me down the walk.
Not knowing how words succeed each other, ghosting
everything, a cat jumps from a low branch

to the roof of a car, to the hood, to the snow,
just like that. But I have kept something
in my pocket—a letter in italic hand

from a daughter who tells, but only a part.
Though she is half a life away, on the desert,
I, old truepenny, go longing after her.


On the street, shapes in the mist swirl up
behind each car, as if wondering, as if
about to follow it. Air breathes and billows,

slurring the ruled lines of clapboarding.
In and out of the mist, children straggle
to the bus stop as my own daughters did,

muffled in blue and green, diminishing
to the far right, where one girl glances back,
her eyes just visible above a foggy scarf.


If this were another medium, a surface
seen at a single glance, I could give myself
to the mist, let omen and recollection be

long strokes laid on with a knife, washed by a fine
smear of white. Without this hushed *and then*,
*and then*, I could love the instant, simply, taking it

at its word. If I had to know, my eye
could follow the steps the cat had daubed in the snow
until they led to the blurred curb and were gone.

# Wise Man

No one here is old enough. The father,
if that's what he is, stands awkward as a stork.
The mother does not know whether to smile
or cry, her face beautiful but ill-defined
as faces of the young are. Even the ass
is a yearling, and the sheep mutter like children.
To whom shall I hand this myrrh that has trailed
a bitter breath after it over the desert?

I am tired of mothers and their milky ways,
of babies sticky as figs. I have left a kingdom
of them. There must be some truth beyond
this sucking and growing and wasting away.
A star should lead an old man, you would think,
to some geometry, some right triangle
whose legs never slip or warp or aspire
to become the hypotenuse. Instead, this star
wandering out of the ecliptic has led us
to dry straw, a stable, oil burning in
a lamp, a mother nursing another mouth.

2

Creation, then, is the only axiom—
and it declines to spell itself across
the sky in Roman letters. Some events
are worth a journey, but there are no
abstract fires or vague births. Each fire
gnaws its own sticks; the welter of what is

conspires in this, a creation you can hold
in your hands, a child. A definite baby
squalls into life, skids out between the legs
of a definite woman, bedded in straw, on the longest
night of the year. And a certain star burns.

# A Dialogue Concerning the Question Whether a Tennis Ball May Be Said to Hanker for the Other Side of the Net

A. Now, for example, when the ball lays its ear
  to the strings of the racket, the moment comes whole.
  Satisfied in the round completion of muscle,
  sun, and rubber, it wishes itself gone
  so that the woman across the net may
  run back, watch the lob float down,
  and drop her brown shoulder for the slam.

B. Let's keep things straight. *You* foresee the tan
  arch of muscles in the far court. The moment
  doesn't care. Feeling is a weed sending
  runners through the roots of the grass. Seized
  at the center, it may be pulled in one stroke,
  leaving the facts: the net, the wood, the woman
  whose footwork you admire are particles in motion.

A. The grain of the wood is desire. If you begin
  extracting, an instant flattens to splotches of color
  on cardboard. Never longing for the stretch
  of a body or a ball singing as the strings
  taught it, the dead present could create
  nothing. Uncaused, uncausing, it would have
  no reason to perish into a new time.

# Headlights

A girl in a Triumph takes the rise and bank
of a mountain road on a rainy night. Her lights
reach for guardrails or catch the sudden white
of dogwood or wrinkled water in the creek.
They are antennae, quivering ahead
of her, naming whatever is to come.
She stops at a turnout, cuts the ignition,
and walks a few yards into the spongy woods,

where dark clings like cobwebs. Now, if she knows,
it is not knowledge of luminous paint edging
the road. She guesses the night's dip and strike.
She hears the roar of her own body, creating
itself, instant by instant, as the trees grow
and steam and sing themselves into fact.

# The Mirror

She draws the fray of his hair, the curtain,
the steaming mug of tea, and in his hand
the broken circles of a bunch of grapes.

Aware that something's missing from the sketch,
she props a mirror on a chair and draws
herself. The pattern in her dress eases

into the patterned tablecloth, and the row
of buttons falling from her throat rhymes
with the hanging grapes. Meanwhile, of course,

they talk, and suck the light green meat of grapes
out of the purple skins, and touch—real figures
against the figured wall. Their hands have weight

and motion scarcely mentioned in the pen's
pure lines. I see it unmistakably—
I, who lean in the doorway, writing a poem.

No, to tell the truth, it is my hair
curling under her pen, the tea warms
my breastbone. I swallow the seeds of grapes

and touch her skin, excited and afraid.

# The Happy Man

The grass comes green with less astonishment
this year, tomatoes ripen to a less
convincing red. He wonders why. The leeks
still shoot their wild tails in the air, and carrots

swell to the moist loam. The soup must be
the same, but somehow it has gone to sleep
on his tongue. He used to believe that happiness
must lie in the perfection of a few

choice goods. But now perfection pales.
Does nature like an envious governor
lay a surtax on the happy man
diminishing his pleasure year by year?

He feels his satisfaction growing tired
even as he admires his favorites,
the bronze chrysanthemums along the walk
that bloom as solid as the heads of nails.

## Poem against Celery Hearts
## and Cream Cheese

When I am hungry enough,
I will gnaw my way to wisdom.
When my famished eyes
turn into mouths, I will
no longer fool myself
with stuffed olives.
I will know what the goat knows.

# Fat

I am the girl who jumped
the Hodgmans' fence
so quick they never saw me.

Skipping rope, I always did
hot peppers. But once on the way home
I got in a strange car.

I screamed and beat on the windows
but they smiled and held me.
They said I could go

when I put on the costume.
So I climbed into it, pulled up
the huge legs, globby

with veins, around my skinny shins,
pulled on this stomach
that flops over itself.

I pushed my arm
past the hanging elbow fat
into the hands and fingers,

tight like a doctor's glove
stuffed with vaseline.
I hooked the top at my neck,

with these two bladders
bulging over my flat chest.
Then I pulled the rubber mask

down over my head and tucked in
the cheek and chin folds,
hiding the seam. I hate

the smell. When they pushed me
out of the car, I slipped
and staggered as if the street

was wet with fish oil.
You see what this costume is.
If you will undo me, if you will

loan me a knife, I will step out
the way I got in. I will run on home
in time for supper.

# Tongue

He did not mean to test the cold
or his own daring. He did it idly,
not thinking, as he might suck
a little solace from his thumb.

Alone at recess, watching three boys
wrestle in the snow, he touched
his tongue to the cyclone fence
and it froze. The cold clanged shut.

With his fingers, he pulled at the tongue
as if it were a leech, sucking
the blood of his leg. But the ice held.
In panic, he tore away his mistake,

tore loose his tongue, leaving skin
like patches of rust on the metal.
What could he do with the torn and swollen
tongue, with shame that tasted like blood?

In school, he hid his mouth behind
his hands. He swallowed. He swallowed.

# A Procession of Ants, Chanting

Words have reason to be sullen.
The corn, tired of the same field,
grows scraggly as teeth, and the sun

hangs in the sycamore tree
like a voice from a loudspeaker, bald
and indecipherable. We who are old,

having foretold the day and hour
of the world's end, now live on,
ridiculous, in a vanished place.

And the young? They have one
ambition: to be doctors.
Long into the night they memorize

the roads to *normal*. So words,
as I say, poke around like ants
in the blown leaves, unable to run.

They drag their thoraxes over the loam
crying how thin the daylight has become
and how debauched the queen. But then

in the routine static of feelers struck
on feelers, comes news of a dead beetle.
They smell the iridescent corpse

shimmering green and gold against
the pale lichen, and they move
toward it, finding the trail.

They mount the hump of a log and there
it is, grand as a yacht, the beetle
beached on its back, its faceted eyes

studying dust, its six legs rising
like antlers. Stumbling but solemn, they hoist
the corpse and bear it—its own bier—

the moving line of ants chanting
for once the old polyphony
of beetle wings above and leafmold

underfoot, the song of the sojourner
returning to his hill, the whole
column keeping the beat, calling
the rich cadence of decay.

# The Woman Who Was Ready to Die

Unmistakably, the picture showed the mound
under her skull fixing its tentacles
in the grey rocks. The doctor circled around
the news, but she had guessed it. A sudden ease
moved through her like the wash of waves. Her grass
would somehow mow itself this summer. Her children
would untangle their own marriages.
There would be no more choices, no more men.

Yet when her face came loose, when her blood forgot
its language, she took up kitchen knives and fought
the squid. She slashed his watery belly, cut
at the fat arms that reached down and undid
the buttons of her body. When he brought
his mouth to hers, she tore his lips, she spat.

# Skier

The eye hails its friends far off: the cone
of the mountain, gradations of white and violet
in the snow, and barely moving against the distant
cold, the blue jacket and green cap of a skier.
Information only, or so the eye supposes.

But smell knows better. In the presence of a fire,
wet leather, wax and coffee, we inhale
feelings. Pleasure and regret sleep in the pungent
wool of a sweater. Wood smoke informs the body,
dropping like a laugh from throat to loins.

The blue-green figure on the slope is closer
than we thought. Her long sweep across
the hypothesis of snow enters here,
with breath and the shaking out of hair.
We take her in, as desire, out of the cold.

## Script for a Cold Christmas

These reds and greens, of course, are all wrong—
the blazing log, the star like a sunflower
almost toppling the tree. All fall, the colors
have been diminshing. Look: the beech tree
breathes twigs of vapor against the grey sky,
icicles drop their spindly light in a long beard
from eaves to bush to ground. My promises
have cracked and dropped away like old bark.
I am a winter stick, a flagpole clanging
a hollow note in the wind. There is nothing
dramatic here, neither jubilation
nor despair, but rather a kind of exile
as when in a foreign country you shrink
into yourself, unable to speak.

Our rituals exaggerate. The star
was no catherine wheel spinning and hissing
over the stable. It was a star, a point
of no dimension, one match flaring across
a frozen lake. The shepherds, hearing the angels'
song, thought it was the wheeze of a cold sheep
it had so thin a sound. They heard but hardly
spoke, saving their words like a last handful
of grain. And the child—one child, not a creche
in every park. This one was different,
but not yet. Now it was a small jug
of flesh with a candle glimmering inside.

It is almost cold enough. The year is shrinking
toward a small festival, a saturnalia

that will fit in the cavity of a tooth.
We may gather up our deaths and make
of them a twig fire, hold our hands
to it, and sing for the cold seed.

from "Mexican Poems" (1984)

*The illustrations in this section are from ancient Mexican clay stamps, used to decorate pottery, cloth, paper, or even one's body. The reproductions are from Jorge Enciso's* Design Motifs of Ancient Mexico.

# The Monkey

In Chiapas, at the edge of the rain,
we begin to feel sick—nothing
violent but an insinuation
in the bowels. Don't drink the water
we tell each other. Don't eat the pork
dripping on spits in the street.
Don't hear the cries, the bells.

But we have come too far. The kites
have sighted us and the nightjars talk
in our sleep. Insects we cannot name
climb up our legs and dig in
at the groin. We were tourists,
we thought, but the pitchy air
has settled in our throats.

On a rained-out road, we come
to the monkey, gesturing, scratching
himself, and shrieking, his muzzy
belly bulging with fruit, his cock
cocked. He dances ahead of us,
a scurvy guide leading his party
of two, deeper and deeper in.

# With Esperanza on the Roof

You're right, Esperanza, the roof is yours,
the concrete tubs under the cockeyed awning,
the wet sheets that you knead like bread,

the line where the sun pounds the clothes
a second time. You're right to wonder what
I'm doing up here, asking about your toothache,

your sister who married the old man, your young
brother who has not been drunk now for a month.
May he continue, we agree. What am I doing

looking out over the valley as though I'd
never seen roofs and domes before, nor the lake
above the dam, its arms out like a lizard

sleeping in the sun. What am I doing
watching the egrets in the clump of trees.
I should know them. All day and all night

they keep a rhythmic pulse, like hoarse crickets
or geese saying their beads. Now they row
their slow white boats across the sky, their legs

trailing. One uncoils its neck, feathers its great
wings, swings its legs forward, hovers, and lands
in the top of a pine tree. Another sweeps around

past us and strokes its way to the lake.
Esperanza, the roof is yours. I'm going down.
Maybe it's not remarkable how thin the air is

after the rain, how brilliant the clouds are.
But look. The wall around the roof is scalloped.
On each peak sits a tough geranium

reaching its stringy stems outward and down,
handing you a crimson knot of bloom.

## Toads

Dusk comes suddenly on the narrow road
that follows the hill eastward and down. The woman's
fears are the live pieces of dark that appear
where there was nothing.

In a tree that had been bare, she sees a dozen
great-tailed grackles slanting like eyebrows.
From a deserted hut comes a black feather of smoke
and a low voice.

Between the rocks, the dark is filling with toads:
their breath is the slow rising of the sky
behind her. She fears rain and she fears the toad-dust
thirsty for rain.

But then the evening sidles up to her,
holding out precious stones in a handkerchief.
She draws away from the opals and tigers' eyes,
sure that she will pay

too much, but he touches her sleeve and she turns.
Below her in the rich light she sees a row
of trees like bubbles of blood welling up
from a cut

and beyond them the sky hunched like a toad
over the town, its skin mottled purple,
black, and vermillion. If this is the dark,
there is no escaping it.

She asks the name of the sky-toad, huge
and lovely. A tongue flickers from his mouth
and now the sun itself is a stone, burning
in his forehead.

# The Moon Seen as a Slice of Pineapple

Tonight an old man follows the narrow streets
turning and returning like a thought.
His hat down, his loose pants flapping,
he looks in at the light of a cantina,

then walks on, wind in a thin body of dust.
He has looked everywhere. Already his sons
are lost and now his daughter has slipped
away, the girl who wakened him like rain.

Five mongrels, bleached by the moon, circle him
and snarl, slouching like thieves. They take him
for a stranger, but he pries a stone from the street.
He has lived here longer than any of them.

He knows where she must be: in the gardens
of the rich, it rains every day. She sits
on the branch of a jacaranda, while a man
with perfect teeth, hardly younger than himself,

holds to her mouth a slice of pineapple.
"Eat," he says as the juice drips from his hand.
She eats and a black dog slides from the shadows
to lick the moonlight falling on her legs.

## Christmas, Mexico

December here, with sun and the faint smell
of wood smoke in the air—
a late September day. The jasmine drops
a few last blooms; limes swell

and ripen, one by one, outside the door.
Dusk comes a little earlier.
Here, we will have months or years to eat
the apple of our hearts down

to the dark seeds. How leisurely the fall.
How slow the holy cold comes on.

# Sonnet

*for Marion*


I didn't care to see the rubbed enamel
or go on burro-back to what's the town
that's covered up by lava? Nor sail down
some muddy lake in a cast-iron pail.
I'd rather read a book or write a poem.
When you come back, I won't regret not seeing
Tarascan dug-out boats or not being
there on the dock to bring the whitefish home.

And here? I'm watching the wind come up, fixing
the sestet of a sonnet, wondering how
you are, with whom, deciding after all
some sights are worth a journey, wondering
if I could catch you there at Pátzcuaro
before you set out for the waterfall.

## The Coyote Flower

Like standing water, the day generates
its own fauna. We are artists, we say,
waking late into the perfect weather.
We walk to the post office and come away

empty. This is the privacy we wanted,
the garden where jasmine hangs overhead
and a finger of light raises the leaves
of vestido de novia to an unearthly red,

a place where we might learn a Benedictine
discipline—how a plot of sun and shade
four yards by four can grow our meat and drink.
We work a little at the stubborn trade.

But now friends come. We welcome them and find
something to eat. Beside one visitor
we see a clumsy flower grow large until
a grinning snout emerges and wet fur—

a small coyote. From the corners of our eyes
we see him bob and crouch behind the lime

tree, snapping at whatever we let fall.
Quick as hunger, he works around the rim

of our slow talk: he smiles, he gestures, he eats.
We wonder why the morning air reneges
on promises, where the time has gone,
what gnawing that might be between our legs.

# The Photographer

It has been raining hard for an hour, and the water, having no
other place to go, roars down over the cobblestones carrying tree
limbs, Pepsi bottles, socks, clumps of alfalfa, the plastic body of a
doll. Drain pipes throw streams of roof-water into the center of the
street. Three children flatten themselves against a door, and a
flatbed truck sloshes slowly up the street like a river steamer.

Now an old woman, head covered by a rebozo, turns the corner
into the full force of the rain. She pauses a minute on the narrow
sidewalk above the cascading water, then steps in cautiously,
starting across. If you don't get *this* picture, you deserve doorways
and sunsets the rest of your life. You grab the Leica from the back
of the chair, make a quick guess about the exposure, and walk out
into the downpour. The woman is hardly fifteen feet from you,
feeling her way on the slick stones, the water piling up against her
heavy skirt, her shoulders curled, her face creased and dripping.
You focus and shoot. As the water surges almost to her knees, she
staggers a step backward, loses her footing, and falls. You shoot.
She sits on one hip in the flood, bracing herself with her left arm,
while the water plunges into her lap and presses her chest. One
of her sandals floats downstream behind her. You shoot. She
clambers up, crouching, one hand in the water ready to catch
herself if she slips again. But she makes it to the curb where you
offer her a hand, help her onto the sidewalk. She pushes past
you, bending into the storm. Why not, you think, and shoot again,
catching her dark shape against the wall. She pauses, steadied, you
like to think, by the clear eye of the Leica.

# The Expatriate

Her northern friends go home when the heat builds
before the rain. Her place is here. Her one
visitor, in these hot months, is the wind
who knocks at her door, stands in the afternoon sun

and knocks and knocks. She doesn't want him in,
yet his knock echoes in the vacancies
of her body. Finally, the kitchen door swings in
and she knows he is back, banging his hat

on his thigh to shake the dust. He rests one haunch
on the table and smiles to welcome himself. She hardly
looks at him and yet he talks unpausing
like the sheet that flaps outside the window.

As she knew he would, he tells her his life,
how he camped out like a goat in the thorny hills,
how nothing there had any give to it—
all rock and cactus closed in on itself.

As he stretches into a chair, his voice mimics
pleasure, and for a moment here in the early
evening, she thinks he might be the real wind,
the wind she remembers blowing off the lake

at home, smelling of fish and pitch. Perhaps
when she looks out in the morning, she will see,
where the road dips, the sumac and box elder
up to their ears in mist. She will carry the oars

down a spongy path to the dock, row out, the center
of all the circles, and dive in the clear water.
But now the wind coughs, and she sees him wipe
dust from the back of his hand. He is not what

she had in mind, this wind that swaggers like
the holy ghost blown in from Guanajuato.
He makes the right gestures, touching her sleeves
and her loose hair. He thinks he'll stay the night.

In the morning, she finds dust everywhere—on sills,
on the tops of her shoes, in cracks between
glazed tiles. As she walks through the still house,
it billows up around her legs like mist.

# The Frog

## 1

Last night, meaning to speak of *chicken soup*,
I spoke instead of *soup of dust*, which might
have been profound but wasn't. Here I become
absurd, an embarrassment—too tall, too pink,
missing the jokes, getting the sexes wrong.
The customs police found my cache of words
and confiscated it; I took a deep breath
at the border, blew it out, and was no one,
a foreign body with a limp. And yet
I keep returning. There's something to it,
this emptiness—as idiots push with a vague
grin through the swinging doors of heaven.

## 2

A man bewitched into a frog, admiring
the calves of passing ladies, can only croak
or hop ridiculously after them.
And yet his thin legs dangle and stretch
voluptuously in the algae, his mouth
relaxes into speechless green. His ear,
which once distinguished shades of condescension
in a woman's voice, now hears only
the slap of water on cypress knees,
the hum of insects asking to be eaten.

## Letter to the North

That's us, naked as frogs in the sunshine,
our thumbs in our ears.
Think of us, thinking of you and grinning.

Somewhere, if we remember right, leaves
have turned. Soon, when daylight
saving goes, night will creep up sleeves

and pant legs, and snow will flutter
onto the stiff grass
like tiny leaflets that demand surrender.

You will submit. There in the Protestant dark
you do not need
to kneel beside a curtained box to speak

the syllables of your confession. The year
performs that rite.
As cold comes on, it strips you to a bare

knuckle, a knot of gristle that must bend,
straighten, and bend,
to keep from freezing. Winter assigns its penance

and you suffer it: in March you are forgiven.
Here, neither Catholic
nor cold, we are happy all year long,

but look at us again. Our mouths, unshriven,
twist with the sweet
of mangos. Our eyes enact their own seasons.

# Explosions at 4:00 A.M.

**1**

Into our alien sleep drop these slow
explosions: *black   black*.
They executed Maximilian not far from here;
are they lining up the foreigners again

to shoot them one by one? Or is some crazed
soldier lobbing grenades over the rim
of the mountain? Maybe it's a celebration,
caps of dynamite struck with a sledge

to mark a saint's day. Esperanza will know—
or perhaps not. In this country, things well up
from underneath: oil, lava, fury and desire
pressed from the fat leaves of ferns.

**2**

I hesitate at the corners of walled streets
and at the place where the road empties
into the bare need of the mountains; I fear
for my daughter absent somewhere in the night.
And now these intimations, as when someone
knocks and knocks at the door, knocks and knocks,
and I delay, hoping the sound will stop.

**3**

Sculptors speak of *negative space*,
the substantial emptiness
that balances what is. Here,

in a strange bed, in the dark,
we lift our hands to feel the loops
between our fingers. Wherever

our bodies leave a cavity
the emptiness sits down and waits.
Explosions: are they the other

heartbeats, the pulse of absence
proving that *its* blood, too, can burst?

4

With a deft
blow, the knife
cracks the shell
of our sleep.
The white runs
and we are exposed,
a double yolk,
two embryos unready.

5

We came here thirty years ago, before
we knew each other. Things were more explicit
then. Bells counted the daylight hours,

and we ourselves were an equation stretching
clear across the page. Now factored down,
we lie in a small bed, saying little.

Numbers, as they move toward zero, catch glimpses
of their ghostly counterparts rising
on the other side. I don't mean death. I mean

a sort of symmetry where slouching darkness
follows like a mime, mocking the solid shapes.

6

The wheels of the DC-9
clanked into the fuselage
like boxcars coupling
    *black    black*
but in the radar-mothered
air above Chicago, we
didn't recognize the sound.

7

Why do we choose
this place, where

the water's suspect
and the people

distant,
where giving up

our words, we
give up subtlety

and ease
and wit? I guess

we come to memorize
our bodies, singly

and together.
The trace of fear

marks out
our arteries.

8

Remember in psychology the white goblet
against the black ground?
All at once the goblet disappears

and two black faces stare nose to nose
across the gap.
Let's say we are the goblet opening

upward in a perfect bowl. We listen
for the explosion:
    *black*   the picture shifts. We strain

to bring the goblet back and hold it, to toast us,
joined and central,
but the faces come again, legitimate

as we are, changing places with us,
dark for light,
along the edges of our body.

## The Cur

**1**

The wild dogs in the road weave and smell
among the stones like dry rivers prowling
for rain. When they are gone, you say,
"They will never find it, whatever it is."

"Even the sun is sick," you say, "eating
that wormy meat on the hillside." In truth,
the sun is feverish, bumping across
the sky on the flat bed of a truck, hoping

to get to the doctor in time. "And there's the moon,
with her teeth gone, waving from her high window."

The rain, we wonder, what has become of the rain?
Weak from amoebas, it crawled away to the coast

and lies in the tangled trees tormented by
mosquitoes. Of the gods, only the wind
is up. He paces from mountain to mountain, torn
by thorns, rubbing handfuls of dust in his hair.

2

With the gods raving or ill, what will we do?
The garden we come back to is beautiful.
The bougainvillaea tosses a crimson scarf
over its shoulder, and pure white irises

catch the light under their skirts. The fronds
of the banana tree wave themselves ragged
in the wind. Within these walls, we water
everything. We watch a tree of avocados

ripen in what is left of the sun. A pair
of kingbirds careen in the wild air, dive,
and mate in flight. We, too, love recklessly,
knowing the moon has seen too much to care.

She watches, faintly, through the blowing branches,
but she cannot remember who we are
nor what warm blood we offered her when she
still had an appetite for sacrifice.

3

Now at dusk the wind dies and an empty air
falls on the stones and petals of the garden.
"Who needs the gods," you say, "and their brass bands."
A bell speaks deep in its throat and, on the road

to Dolores, we hear the barking of a dog,
faint and insistent. Another answers
and another. As dark comes down, the howl
blows from the north, gathering voices: mongrels

snarling through the fences of their teeth
and German shepherds, frantic, as night itself
picks the lock. The noise swirls through the street,
a relentless coughing, the breath of dogs spreading

like an infection. Now on the roof next door,
a huge cur stands against the sky. He lunges
over us, eyes white as stone, his fury
standing in spikes along the hump of his spine.

*The Lagoon* (1989)

*The bird and insect figures in this section are reproductions of wood engravings made by Takeshi Takahara for the original limited edition of* The Lagoon, *a collaborative book handmade by Timothy Barrett, Janet Lorence, Bonnie Stahlecker, and Takeshi Takahara.*

# Papermaker

Tired. She was up at 5:00
using the vat before it got
cluttered with talk—

tough rag sheets couched
and pressed, and the fine kozo
thin as breath

on a cold day. Battering plants
so words can have a place
to lie down.

# The Heron

The great
blue heron lives
by stepping
slowly and
standing still,
letting the ideas
come to him.

# The Moult

When the cicada's skeleton
unzips at the thorax,
when he steps out of his skin
and reels in the new air,
can we say he feels joy—
as we do
when we hear the old fabric
split across our backs
and the moult begins?

# Sheets

Tomorrow the sheets will come
from the press moist
and sweet as skin.
Those are the best times:
going to bed
and peeling out in the morning
like waves on the lagoon,
barely perceptible, barely
lifting from the deep
and weedy night.

## The Facts

Beneath the curve
of the canoe move
the grandfatherly grasses
spelling out the facts
with their great loops
and ascenders, an alphabet
only the carp can read.

## The Carp

Below the weeds swims
the carp himself,
the professor
whose thoughts rise
in slow bubbles and
burst, spreading
a grave mist
over the lagoon.

## Talk on the Porch

Under the wingbeats of moths,
under the flight
of griefs and exaltations

which circle recklessly
and alight, calm
as evening, on the screen,

under the talk
lies the air itself,
the translucent sheet

on which our voices
write with a dry brush.

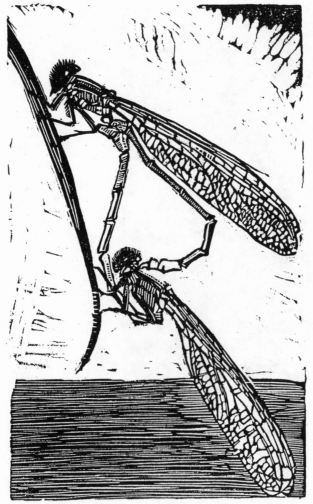

# The Fossil

On the smooth limestone, a man etches
the wings of a dragonfly,
the bulging eyes, the abdomen
thin as bamboo.
The stone insect hovers and stares
out of the Mesozoic.

# Ceremony

Here is the slow history
of the dunes: tough grasses
delaying the sand till poplars
and pines can hold it. Then oaks
and maples, and in a hundred years
the deep beech and hemlock,
the climax forest, where the wood
thrush sings. The inquiries,
the ceremonious courtship,
the dark and fragrant temple.

# The Iowa Poetry Prize Winners

1987

Elton Glaser, *Tropical Depressions*

Michael Pettit, *Cardinal Points*

1988

Mary Ruefle, *The Adamant*

Bill Knott, *Outremer*

1989

Terese Svoboda, *Laughing Africa*

Conrad Hilberry, *Sorting the Smoke*